D1029657

Celebrities
with
♥ Heart

Tim McGRAW

Celebrity with Heart

Sara McIntosh Wooten

Enslow Publishers, Inc.
40 Industrial Road
Box 398
Berkeley Heights, NJ 07922
USA

http://www.enslow.com

Copyright © 2011 by Sara McIntosh Wooten

All rights reserved.

No part of this book may be reproduced by any means
without the written permission of the publisher.

Library of Congress Cataloging-in-Publication Data

Wooten, Sara McIntosh.
    Tim McGraw : celebrity with heart / Sara McIntosh Wooten.
        p. cm. — (Celebrities with heart)
    Includes bibliographical references, index, and discography.
    Summary: "A biography of American country singer Tim McGraw"—Provided
        by publisher.
    ISBN-13: 978-0-7660-3405-1
    1. McGraw, Tim—Juvenile literature. 2. Country musicians—United States—
        Biography—Juvenile literature. I. Title.
    ML3930.M38W66 2010
    782.421642092—dc22
    [B]
                                                                2009023809

ISBN-13: 978-1-59845-207-5 (paperback)

Printed in the United States of America

052010 Lake Book Manufacturing, Inc., Melrose Park, IL

10 9 8 7 6 5 4 3 2 1

To Our Readers: We have done our best to make sure all Internet Addresses in this book were active and appropriate when we went to press. However, the author and the publisher have no control over and assume no liability for the material available on those Internet sites or on other Web sites they may link to. Any comments or suggestions can be sent by e-mail to comments@enslow.com or to the address on the back cover.

Every effort has been made to locate all copyright holders of material used in this book. If any errors or omissions have occurred, corrections will be made in future editions of this book.

♻ Enslow Publishers, Inc., is committed to printing our books on recycled paper. The paper in every book contains 10% to 30% post-consumer waste (PCW). The cover board on the outside of each book contains 100% PCW. Our goal is to do our part to help young people and the environment too!

Illustration Credits: Associated Press, pp. 1, 9, 11, 15, 20, 47, 48, 65, 75, 77, 84, 92, 100, 105, 109, 111; Brian Rasic/Rex USA/courtesy Everett Collection, Inc., p. 58; Michael Bush/UPI/Landov, p. 4; Michael Germana/Everett Collection, Inc., p. 70; Paul Drinkwater/©NBC/courtesy Everett Collection, Inc., p. 94; Sam Jordan/Everett Collection, Inc., p. 44; Time & Life Pictures/Getty Images, p. 32; 20th Century Fox Film Corp. All rights reserved./courtesy Everett Collection, Inc., p. 107; © Universal/courtesy of Everett Collection, Inc., p. 96.

Cover Illustration: Associated Press.

Contents

A Chance Encounter

Tug McGraw, famous baseball pitcher and father of country music hopeful Tim McGraw, sat at a dinner in Philadelphia, Pennsylvania. It was 1991. Tug was there to celebrate with his team, the Philadelphia Phillies, and their World Series win over Kansas City ten years earlier. Tug was known as a party guy. He was always kidding around and looking for a good time.[1] And this night would be no different. But for his son, the evening, along with his father's gift for gab, would change Tim McGraw's life forever.

Seated beside Tug for dinner that evening was a man named Bruce Wendell, a longtime Phillies fan. The two men did not know each other, but during the course of the evening, with normal dinner party chitchat, they learned each other's background.

Tim McGraw was nowhere near Philadelphia that night. He was back home in Nashville, Tennessee. He had dropped out of Northeast Louisiana University two years earlier. Since then, he, along with thousands of other country music hopefuls, had flocked to Nashville, the capital of country music. And along with all the others, McGraw had been scraping around, trying to survive until he could get his big break in the music business. For most, that break would never come.

An easy going, friendly kind of guy, McGraw had no trouble meeting other country musicians in Nashville. Over time, he used his contacts to put a band together. Then he went about trying to book engagements, or gigs, at local bars and restaurants. McGraw's days were spent working at whatever mindless job he could find. But at night he took every opportunity he could to perform with his band. Hopefully, somehow, he would be discovered by an agent, get the break he needed, and his career would begin. Still, after two years, there had been no big breaks for Tim McGraw. And as time moved forward, it was easy to become discouraged.

But things were about to pick up for McGraw, big time. Back in Philadelphia, it turned out that Bruce

A Tough Time in Nashville

For Tim McGraw, it was a tough life. It meant believing in himself against all odds. It meant knocking on doors of agents and recording companies, only to be turned away. To get to Nashville, he had sold pretty much everything he owned, including his car. He had hoped he would quickly be discovered, record an album, and be on his way to fame and fortune. But it did not work like that. Even though McGraw had singing talent, could play the guitar, and had a great look, he was new to Nashville. Doors did not automatically open for him.

Wendell, sitting next to McGraw's father, Tug, worked for a major recording company in Nashville called Curb Records. Not a shy man, Tug quickly saw that his chance meeting with Wendell might be a good thing for his son. He offered to drive Wendell back to his hotel after dinner was over. Wendell agreed. And once in his car, Tug quickly slipped his son's demo tape into the car's sound system.

Wendell was impressed with what he heard. He agreed to take the demo tape back with him to Nashville. And he was true to his word. Once others at Curb Records listened to McGraw's tape, they also liked his sound. McGraw actually might be someone they would want to sign to record for their label.

It would take another year, but in 1993, Curb Records released Tim McGraw's first album, *Tim McGraw*. It would be the first of many during his amazing rise to superstardom. Wendell's instincts had been right—McGraw would bring fame and fortune not only to himself but also to Curb Records.

Yet McGraw's career did not immediately skyrocket. That first album was not a big success. Still, the people at Curb were confident in McGraw's potential. They were not ready to let him go yet. And their confidence paid off. McGraw's second album, *Not a Moment Too*

Tim McGraw performs at the 2009 Academy of Country Music Artist of the Decade All-Star Concert honoring George Strait. McGraw is a huge country star now, but it took many years of hard work to get to the top.

Soon, sold well. Finally he was getting the attention he and Curb Records were looking for.

After that, McGraw's success only continued to build. By the end of 2008, he had released eleven albums and had won countless awards for his music. On top of that, his professional success has been enhanced by personal happiness. In 1996, he and fellow country-music singer Faith Hill were married. Together they have had several record-breaking concert tours, with fans cheering them on as "Mr. and Mrs. New Country Music." The life they have built together shows their devotion to each other as a couple and to their family, as well as to their careers.

Today Tim McGraw is at the top of his professional and personal game. Yet he still maintains a down-to-earth quality, which endears him to his fans.[2] His success does not seem to have gone to his head or turned him into a self-absorbed star. Rather, he takes his fame in stride, loves what he does, and maintains his reputation as a family man.

Beyond family and career, McGraw has yet another focus. He and his wife are committed to using their wealth and fame to help people in need. McGraw serves on the board of the Red Cross as a celebrity representative. He also holds a concert each year in Louisiana to raise money for people in need. And when Hurricane Katrina hit the southern United States in August 2005,

Tim McGraw and fellow Grammy Award–winning country singer Faith Hill have been happily married since 1996. Unlike many other famous couples, they have managed to successfully balance their professional and personal lives.

McGraw headlined a huge concert with other music celebrities, with the money from the concert going to help Katrina victims.

Perhaps Tim McGraw did not need his father's help that night in Philadelphia in order to get his career going. Sooner or later, he might have found his own break. But Tug McGraw's pitch to Bruce Wendell got the job done, and millions of country music fans are happier for it.

Growing Up Timmy

Samuel Timothy McGraw was born on May 1, 1967, in the tiny Louisiana town of Delhi. He was the first child born to his young mother, Elizabeth Ann D'Agostino, whom everyone called Betty. Tim's father was Frank Edwin "Tug" McGraw, Jr. A professional baseball player, Tug and Betty had dated for a few months in 1966. He was twenty-two; she was just eighteen. At that time, Betty's parents were divorced. She was living with her mother and younger sister in Jacksonville, Florida. Tug was in Jacksonville playing baseball for a minor-league team called the Jacksonville Suns.

Shortly after Betty's relationship with Tug was over, her parents decided to try their marriage again. So Betty and her family moved to Winnsboro, Louisiana. By that time, Betty knew she was pregnant.

Her baby's father, Tug McGraw, had moved on. From Florida he had gone to New York to play for the professional baseball team, the New York Mets. He had no idea he had fathered a son with Betty.

For her part, Betty was determined to keep her pregnancy a secret. A slim young woman, she was able to hide her condition from her family for several months by wearing loose-fitting tops. She was embarrassed and knew her family would be disappointed in her if they discovered the truth. But after six months, Betty's mom figured out what was going on.

Once she learned that her daughter was pregnant and who the baby's father was, Betty's mother was outraged. Who was this cocky baseball player who had ruined her daughter's life? He needed to take responsibility for his actions.

But Tug was not interested in taking responsibility. When Betty's mom called him and told him he was soon to be a father, Tug was shocked. After all, as a handsome baseball player, he had had many brief relationships with young women when his team played games in cities around the country.

Tim McGraw's father, New York Mets pitcher Tug McGraw, in 1971.

And how could Betty be sure the baby was his? He certainly was not. Maybe this was a scam to blackmail him so he would pay money to keep Betty and her mother quiet. Because if the media got wind of him having a baby when he was not married to the baby's mother, his career as an up-and-coming baseball player might be tarnished. Maybe even ruined.

15

But Betty's mother had no patience with Tug's excuses. She told him she expected him to do the right thing. She wanted him to marry her daughter. But Tug was not about to do that. He told her he wanted nothing to do with Betty or her child and that they should never try to contact him again. As Tug would later write: "In my own selfish way, it was easier to deny [my fatherhood] than to confront [it]."[1]

Upon learning of her mother's telephone conversation with Tug, Betty was upset and hurt. She felt betrayed and used. But she was determined to raise their child. In fact, as she would later write, she "wanted him to grow up to be 'somebody' just to show Tug McGraw."[2]

As a young mother with no husband, Betty's life was especially hard. Back in those days, her situation was considered disgraceful. She had long dreamed of becoming a professional dancer. But with a baby, that dream was over. On top of that, her family was very poor.

Betty took a part-time factory job, along with a second job as a waitress at a local diner. In the meantime, Betty's parents divorced again. She, along with her mother and younger sister, moved into a tiny apartment in Rayville, Louisiana. There, Betty found another job as a waitress at the local bus station café.

To get to her job on time, Betty had to get up at 4:00 in the morning. Having no car, she walked to work.

Sometimes she would take her baby with her in a stroller. She called him Timmy. He would play in his playpen at work until her younger sister, Regina, could pick him up and take him home to care for him there. Still, despite everything, for the most part Betty was happy. She loved her little son and enjoyed rocking him and singing to him when she was not at work.[3]

Betty was not only pretty, she also had a friendly, easy-going personality. Over time, she came to know her regular customers at the café pretty well. One of them, Horace Smith, took a special liking to her.

Horace was an unmarried truck driver who was single and lonely. He knew Betty was not married and that her life as a single mom was pretty hard. So he began asking her out on dates. Horace was eleven years older than Betty. She was not very interested in dating him, but he persisted. Plus, Betty's mother encouraged her to date Horace. She thought a relationship would be a good thing for her daughter. If she and Horace ended up getting married, Timmy would have a father figure in his life, and Betty would have more security.[4]

Meanwhile, Timmy's father, Tug, was doing very well. His career as a baseball pitcher had taken off. Betty followed his progress by reading newspaper articles about him. And she was resentful. Here he was with growing fame and fortune, while she was living with his son in poverty.[5] It did not seem fair. On top of that, she read one day that Tug was engaged to be married. The news hit her hard.[6] She finally had to accept the fact that Tug wanted nothing to do with her—that she and their son meant nothing to him.

Over time, Betty agreed to go out with Horace. She enjoyed his company, and he was kind to her and to her son. Before long, Betty accepted Horace's marriage proposal. Although she was not in love, she knew that he was a good man and could provide a more stable home life for her and her son.[7] With Horace's job, Betty could also quit her job and stay home to take care of her baby. The opportunity was too tempting to pass up.

Once married, the little family moved to Start, Louisiana. As McGraw would describe it later, "It's just a farming community—cotton, beans, rice. But there's a lot of good, salt-of-the-earth people there who value family. It was a great place to grow up."[8]

As Timmy got older, Betty kept the truth about his real father a secret. She wanted to wait until her son was old enough to understand before he found out. So for the time being, Timmy was known as Timmy Smith instead of Timmy McGraw.

Life settled in for the Smith family. But even with Horace's steady job, they did not have much money. They lived in a small apartment with no telephone and only had Horace's truck to drive. When Horace was away from home on a truck run, Betty had to walk if she needed to go anywhere.

Horace also had high expectations for his young wife. He thought she should have a hot dinner on the table for him when he got home from work. He also expected her to take care of everything he needed when he was at home.[9]

And then, there was his temper. Sometimes, Horace would get so mad at Betty that he would hit her. Sometimes he hit her so hard he knocked her to the floor. And the problem was worse when Horace had been drinking alcohol.[10]

Despite their problems, the Smith family grew over time. In September 1968, Timmy's first half sister was born, Tracey Catherine Smith. Three years later, she was joined by a second little sister, Sandra Estelle Smith.

The Smith family also moved frequently. In fact, they lived in ten different homes in their eight and a half years of marriage. Still, despite the downsides of her life, Betty was grateful to Horace for letting her stay home with her children and be a full-time mother. That made it possible for her to develop a close relationship with each of them.[11]

When Timmy was still a little boy, Horace had a side job taking care of a horse farm. It was a great place for

McGraw's sister Sandra (left), his mother, Betty, and nephew Matthew stand with him as he receives his star on the Hollywood Walk of Fame on October 17, 2006.

Timmy to play. Soon Horace taught him how to ride horses. First he learned to ride on a Shetland pony. But later he graduated to full-size horses. Timmy loved riding and pretending he was a cowboy.[12]

Once he was old enough to start elementary school, Timmy discovered two more passions—music and sports. He was a talented singer. His first performance was singing "The Battle Hymn of the Republic" for a school program when he was in the second grade. Then he got more on-stage experience the next year. He won the part of Winthrop in a town production of *The Music Man*. (That role was played by a young Ronnie Howard in the movie version.) To play the part, Timmy not only had to learn his lines and sing—he also had to talk with a lisp.

Horace was not happy with Timmy's celebrity. Rehearsals were at 5:30 in the evening, which upset his dinner routine. But Betty stood up to Horace and stuck to her guns to give her son this opportunity.[13]

At the same time, Timmy found that he was also a good athlete. He especially loved playing baseball. Like many young boys, he followed professional baseball and collected baseball cards. Little did he know that his card of Tug McGraw, posted on a wall in his room, was a photograph of his real father.

Horace sometimes took Timmy with him on trucking runs carrying cottonseed between Louisiana and Texas. While they traveled,

"By the time I was six, I felt as if I knew the words to every album Merle Haggard ever recorded."

Horace introduced Timmy to country music. McGraw later described his early knowledge of country music by

Merle Haggard: From Inmate to Country Star

Merle Haggard is a country-music legend. After several stints in prison, he was inspired by country singer Johnny Cash, whom he heard perform at San Quentin State Prison in California. While in prison, Haggard got his high school diploma and joined the prison's band. After his final release from prison in 1960, Haggard got a recording contract with Tally Records. His first big hit, "Sing a Sad Song," was released in 1964.

saying, "By the time I was six, I felt as if I knew the words to every album Merle Haggard ever recorded."[14] At the same time, Betty was also a music fan. She enjoyed listening to rock music, including the Beatles and the Beach Boys. So Timmy grew up hearing and learning to love all kinds of music. That broad exposure would influence his singing style as he grew older.

While money was still tight, life at the Smith home seemed to be going fairly well. But when Betty was twenty-seven, she was diagnosed with breast cancer. With three young children, it was a very scary time for her and her family. But with surgery, she recovered quickly and became a cancer survivor.

Still, alone in the hospital for her treatments, Betty had time to think about her life. She began to realize that Horace's temper was having a big impact not only on her but on her children. Timmy had become nervous and just tried to stay out of Horace's way. Tracey was shy and withdrawn. And Sandy often had stomachaches.[15]

Betty had put up with the situation for years. But by 1976, she had had enough. After a particularly violent episode, Horace knocked Betty down and tried to hit her with a chair. And for the first time, she fought back. She attacked Horace, hitting him with a soda bottle. Then she grabbed her children, put them in a car her mother had helped her buy, and drove away. Soon, she filed for divorce.[16]

Despite everything going against her, Betty refused to give up. Her three children were the center of her life. She was determined to keep them with her and to build a new life. Even though her family had little money to live on, she made the best of it for her children, raising them with kindness, care, love, and laughter.

She managed to get a loan and move herself and her children into a home with three bedrooms. To support her family, she took two waitressing jobs. Then she got her high school diploma by going to night school two nights a week. After that, she enrolled as a night student in business school. Her goal was to become a bookkeeper, a job that would bring in more money than waitressing. And bookkeepers worked during the day, when her children were in school.

It took several years, but with hard work and determination, Betty achieved her goals. By the time her son was eleven years old, she had, indeed, landed a good job as a bookkeeper. She kept track of income, payroll, and expenses for a restaurant. And it was one day when she was at her bookkeeping job that Betty got a call from her son that would turn their lives upside down.

A Secret Revealed

Betty picked up the telephone, at first delighted to hear her son's voice on the other end of the line. But her delight soon turned to dismay. Tim was upset—very upset. His voice trembled, and he was near tears. As Betty quickly focused her concern on her son, she heard the words that she had dreaded hearing since he had been born eleven years before.

Like so many other kids his age, Tim had been looking in his mother's closet for hidden Christmas presents. He was hoping to discover toys and games that were not yet wrapped. What he found, however, was something very different. Something that would shock and confuse him.

In his search for hidden gifts, he came upon a piece of paper. A paper his mother had hidden from him all those years—his birth certificate. A birth certificate is a legal record. It lists where a child was born, how much they weighed at birth, how long they were, and the names of their parents. In looking over his birth certificate, Tim was shocked to see "Frank Edwin 'Tug' McGraw" recorded as his father. How could that be true? Tim's father was Horace Smith. After all, he had always been known as Timmy Smith. What was going on?

On top of that, Tim knew who Tug McGraw was. He was a famous baseball pitcher for the New York Mets. Tim even had Tug's baseball card on his wall. Could he possibly be the son of the famous athlete?

Confused and in disbelief, Tim called his mother. He could not wait until she came home from work that evening to talk to her about what he had found. He was so upset he begged her to come home immediately. And, of course, Betty did. But she hardly knew what she would tell her son or how she could explain what he had found.

Betty had always planned to tell Tim the truth about his father. But not when he was just eleven years old. That was too young to be able to understand and to deal with it. Yet, her careful plan fell apart that afternoon.

A Secret Revealed

Betty spent the rest of the day with Tim, telling him about her brief relationship with Tug. It seemed too much for an eleven-year-old to handle. First he had to come to grips with the fact that Horace was not his real father. Then he had to handle the fact that Tug wanted nothing to do with him. That was very hard. But on top of all that, Tim now had to process the fact that his real father was a famous baseball player. That part was fantastic!

Before long, Tim told Betty he wanted to meet his father. But Betty was not sure. After all, Tug had made it very clear that he wanted nothing to do with Betty or Tim. Still, Tim was insistent, and Betty thought he had the right to meet his dad if he wanted to.

So she called Tug, finding him through the office of the Philadelphia Phillies, for whom he was then playing. By this time Tug had been married for nine years and had two children with his wife.

When he got Betty's call, Tug was quite annoyed. He had hoped he was through with her for good. But after discussing the situation with his wife, Phyllis, they decided Tug should go ahead and meet Tim. After all, he was a young boy and very confused. It was the least Tug could do.

They made a plan to meet in Houston, Texas, where the Phillies were to be playing soon. Betty borrowed a car to drive her ecstatic son the three hundred fifty miles from Louisiana to Houston. She was doing all she could to support her son. But she was very nervous about how the meeting with Tug would go.

In addition, Betty had fears of her own. What if Tug met Tim and wanted custody of him? After all, he was a great kid. She knew Tim loved her, but what eleven-year-old would not want to live with a rich baseball hero?[1] As it turned out, she need not have worried.

They met in the lobby of Tug's hotel. Even after twelve years, it was not too hard for Tug to recognize Betty.[2] Betty left her son with his father to chat by themselves. They had hamburgers and milk shakes for lunch and talked sports. Even so, while the visit was cordial, it was not the warm reunion Tim was hoping for. Tug still refused to believe that Tim was really his son. Tug later wrote: "I always thought that it was possible that I was Tim's dad, but I had just ignored it and hoped it would go away."[3] He told Tim it would be better for him to call Tug his friend rather than his dad. He had tickets for Tim and Betty to see the game against the Houston Astros that

> **"I always thought that it was possible that I was Tim's dad, but I had just ignored it and hoped it would go away."**

Name Change

Tim had bragged to his friends at school that he was Tug McGraw's son. But no one believed him. Sometimes arguments led to taunts and fights. For a while, Tim changed his name at school to Tim McGraw. But once he realized his father wanted nothing to do with him, he changed it back to Tim Smith.

day, and he gave Tim an autographed baseball. But when they parted, Tug had no intention of ever seeing Tim or Betty again.

Tim left Houston crushed. He desperately wanted Tug to treat him like he was his son. But Tug refused. Betty did her best to comfort her son, but it was tough. After that, Tim wrote to Tug several times, and he tried to call him on the telephone. But Tug never responded.

Years later Tug would reflect, "In a lifetime of mistakes, this is the one I feel worst about making—and the one I'd most like to go back to and correct."[4]

Despite his identity crisis, Tim remained an excellent student throughout school. As he grew older, he was outstanding at baseball, football, and basketball. He was also active in 4-H. It is an organization that encourages kids to learn about farming, animals, good citizenship, and healthy living. Tim also enjoyed singing in high school. He had a big talent and sang in the school choir.

He also put his horse-riding skills to work by riding in school rodeos. After years of practice, he had become a very good rider. Betty had forbidden him to ride in a professional rodeo because she knew it was a very dangerous sport. But one time, he signed her name on an entry application and entered. Needless to say, he came home bruised and scuffed up pretty badly. That was the last of his professional rodeo days.

As a growing teen, Tim also had another hidden talent. He was a businessman. He figured out that he could take his weekly allowance, pay his sisters to do his chores for him, and still make a profit for doing nothing. He was smart. He knew he did not want the life of most Monroe, Louisiana, kids. They usually ended up with a job at a local factory. No, his goal was to be a millionaire before he turned thirty years old.[5]

A Secret Revealed

By the time he graduated from Monroe Christian High School in 1985, Tim had earned the second highest grades of any of his classmates. So with high school behind him, Tim set his sights toward college. Still, he was not quite sure what he wanted to do. For a while, he thought of becoming a lawyer. Then he decided he would make a career in sports medicine. Regardless, he was ready to enroll at Northeast Louisiana University in Monroe.

The big problem was how to pay for college. Even going to a local university, it would cost a lot more money than Betty could manage.

It was Tim who suggested that Betty call Tug for help. Tug had recently announced he was retiring from baseball. So now the way was clear—even if the media found out about Tim, it would not hurt Tug's career.

So Betty wrote to Tug for help with Tim's college expenses. When he did not write back, she decided to get legal help. She had a lawyer send Tug papers saying that he owed Betty $350,000 in back child support, since he had never paid her a cent for Tim's care.

The legal notice got Tug's attention. Even though he still refused to believe Tim was really his son and there was no proof, he decided to settle the issue of financial support out of court. He agreed to pay for Tim's college expenses. In exchange, he insisted that neither Tim nor

Tim McGraw (left) with his father in 1994. After years of denial, Tug finally accepted Tim as his own after Tim graduated high school. Their relationship as father and son would continue to grow.

Betty ever contact him again. He also demanded that Tim never use McGraw as his last name.

Tim was hesitant. He insisted on seeing Tug one more time before he signed those papers. Tug agreed to meet Tim in Houston. And as it turned out, the meeting would change both men's lives. Upon seeing Tim as a young man, Tug immediately saw the resemblance between himself and Tim. Even Tug's agent was convinced of their connection. Tug later wrote: "[I]t was as if I was looking at a picture of myself twenty years earlier."[6]

And for the first time, Tug actually gave Tim his full attention. The two played tennis together and had dinner that evening. Tim told Tug all he wanted was "someone he could call Dad who knew [he] was his dad."[7] And Tug responded, "From that point on, I was Tim's dad and he was my son."[8]

A Change of Plans

Tim McGraw headed off to Northeast Louisiana University in Monroe, Louisiana (now called the University of Louisiana at Monroe), in the fall of 1985. He had accepted a singing scholarship from the university. That, along with his father's financial assistance, would pay for his education. Tim McGraw's future looked bright.

But his education goals would not work out. Sure, he had been an excellent student in high school. But once on the college campus, Tim turned his attention to his social life rather than to his studies. He remembered his college days as majoring in "happy hour." By that he meant he was more interested in partying than he was in applying himself to his studies.[1]

Tim also joined a men's social fraternity, or club, called Pi Kappa Alpha. Like many college freshmen, he was spreading his wings. But his freedom from home under Betty's watchful eye seemed more than he was ready to handle.

Based on his lack of effort and interest, McGraw's college grades were not good. He soon realized that a law degree was probably not a realistic goal.[2] So he turned to sports medicine as his backup career goal.

At the same time, Tim's love of music persisted. He bought a used guitar at a pawn shop for twenty-five dollars. Then he taught himself to play. He focused on learning the chords for songs he had grown up hearing on truck runs with Horace, along with some of Betty's rock favorites. But learning to play the guitar was not easy—especially for Tim's fraternity brothers. He drove them crazy with hours upon hours of bad chords. According to Tim, his roommate sometimes hid his guitar so they could get some peace and quiet.[3]

In the meantime, Tim had little contact with his father since that last time together in Houston. In fact, Tug declined an invitation to Tim's high school graduation, much to Tim's disappointment. But in the spring of 1986, Tug called Tim and suggested that he come to

Florida during his college spring break. He wanted Tim to meet his wife and children who would be vacationing there. Tim was thrilled with the idea. And while it could have been a very uncomfortable time, everyone rallied, got along well, and had a great time.[4]

Meanwhile, Betty and her two daughters decided to move from Louisiana back to Jacksonville, Florida. And when his first year of college was over, Tim decided to join them. Once in Jacksonville, he enrolled at a community college there so he could continue to work on getting his college degree.

During his spare time, Tim began playing his guitar and singing with local bands in the Jacksonville area. Even though he was a bit shy about performing at first, he came to enjoy it. And his confidence began to build.[5]

"If you sing as good as you look, you'll make it in country music."

While in Jacksonville, Tim happened to meet country music great Randy Travis. Tim was working in a restaurant where Travis and his manager were eating one day. Once Tim realized they were in the restaurant, he knew he had to take advantage of the opportunity. He introduced himself to them and told them of his growing thoughts of having a career in country music.

Why Nashville?

Nashville, Tennessee, was, and still is, the clear capital of the country-music world. For years it had been the home of the Grand Ole Opry, which began as a country-music radio station in 1925. At that time, the station highlighted country-music bands with such names as "The Fruit Jar Drinkers," "Fiddling Arthur Smith," and "The Gully Jumpers." These groups played music that had become popular in the southern United States and the Appalachian Mountains. It was known as hillbilly music.

Over the years, country music continued to grow and change. It began to pull from a variety of different kinds of music—blues, gospel, and folk, to name a few. In addition, new band instruments were added. Moving from fiddles, harmonicas, and cider jugs, country-music bands expanded to include drums and electric guitars.

He wanted their advice as to what he should do to pursue that dream. Travis told him without hesitation that he needed to move to Nashville, Tennessee. And as Travis's manager told him, "If you sing as good as you look, you'll make it in country music."[6]

Tim did not act immediately on Randy Travis's advice. Instead, he decided to move back to Monroe, Louisiana, and go back to school there. He also started his own band, called the Electones. The band played the songs Tim had grown up with—older songs made famous by such country music giants as Merle Haggard and George Jones. They also played newer country songs by such bands as the Eagles, the Little River Band, and the Allman Brothers. With practice, the Electones developed a mix of traditional country and rock.

But as time went by, Tim finally decided he did, indeed, want to follow up on Travis's advice. It would be a huge risk, but he wanted to try his luck in Nashville. As Travis had pointed out, if singing country music was his dream, Nashville was the place to be.

Of course, Tim was just one of thousands of country-music hopefuls with the same idea. The odds of him making it in Nashville were overwhelmingly against him—kind of like winning the lottery. But he was ready to try.

Betty stood behind her son's decision. She was clearly aware of the risks. But she knew this was what her son wanted with all his heart. Still, leaving college was a big decision. Completing his education would surely open doors for Tim. Instead, by going to Nashville, he was choosing a long shot—a very long shot. But Betty believed that if her son did not try his luck in Nashville, he would always look back and regret it. And if things did not work out, he could always go back to school.[7] Tim was a bit more lighthearted about his choice. As he would later say, "[E]ven though it was scary, I wasn't giving up much. I thought I could make it."[8]

Besides Betty, Tim also consulted his father, Tug, for advice about quitting college and going to Nashville. Unlike Betty, Tug was not encouraging. He strongly felt that his son should finish his college education. But Tim had a ready comeback for his father. He reminded Tug that he had abandoned his college education to pursue his career in baseball. Tug could hardly argue with that!

So Tim sold practically everything he owned, including his car, his shotguns, and his water skis, to get some cash to live on in Nashville until he could find a job there. Without a car, he got to Nashville on a Greyhound bus. He arrived on May 9, 1989. Although it would take more time than he expected, that was the first day of a whole new life for Tim McGraw.

5

Building a Career

Once in Nashville, Tim McGraw quickly found an apartment and a roommate. After that, he began a series of odd jobs just to earn enough money to survive. For one, he took a job cleaning and repairing grocery store shopping carts for a while. At the same time, he also found some restaurants and pubs that would let him sing in the evenings when he was not working. He even took singing jobs that paid nothing, just to get some exposure and more experience. His hope was that someone—some music agent or someone with connections in the music industry—would hear him and champion him with a recording company.

Building a Career

Over time, McGraw pulled a band together and headed out on the road. Tug helped pay for a van the band could ride in and a U-Haul trailer for their equipment. They canvassed the southern and southwestern United States playing wherever they could to get noticed.

McGraw also used his home-grown business experience to help the band. They bought some cheap silk roses, which they sold at a profit to the people who came to hear them perform. But as they sang, a lot of the women in the audience would throw the roses onto the stage. So once their performance was over, the band simply collected the stray roses and got them ready to sell again at their next performance. It was not a big source of income, but it helped.

Still, despite McGraw's efforts and hard work, nothing changed for him. He continued the same grueling pattern of working odd jobs during the day and singing at night. After two years in Nashville, Tim McGraw had no big break to show for his efforts.

One thing he needed to help his career move forward was to make a demo tape that would showcase his singing talent. It would be a calling card that he could take to recording studios in Nashville. Of course, the recording studios got lots of demo tapes from all sorts of bands and singers. So even with a demo tape, his chances of success would still be a long shot. But with luck, it might be a way to get noticed.

The problem was, recording a demo tape took money, which McGraw did not have. But finally, a friend loaned him three thousand dollars so he could get a tape recorded. For McGraw, it would turn out to be a loan well worth taking.

That was the demo tape McGraw's father, Tug, had his dinner friend, Bruce Wendell, listen to in Philadelphia in 1991. And he was impressed. So he took it to Curb Records and suggested they give McGraw some attention. It would be the turning point in McGraw's career. Curb executives heard the tape and realized they might have a profitable talent in Tim McGraw. They were willing to take a risk and sign him to record for them. Tug McGraw would later write: "I believe it was fate that put Bruce Wendell at my table that night—it was meant to be, for Tim. Finally, after years of disappointment and rejection, Tim was actually able to benefit from being my son."[1]

Signing with Curb Records was McGraw's dream come true. Finally he had the break he needed to move his career forward! And like many artists with their first contracts, he thought his future was secured. The rest of the road to fame and fortune would surely be a piece of cake.

But as he soon found out, even with a contract, his career goals were not assured. Like many new artists, he still had a lot of hurdles and hard work ahead of him.

Curb signed a contract with McGraw to record his first album. But putting together an album was a big deal. First of all, McGraw did not write his own songs. So his first task was to listen to hundreds of demo tapes from various songwriters. Then he had to pick the songs he thought would work well for him and become hits for the album. It was a tricky and time-consuming process.

It was also a group process, which made it even harder. Curb Records had a huge stake in the McGraw album, and it was not about to set him loose to pick songs all by himself. One important player in that process was a man named Byron Gallimore, a record producer for Curb Records. As they worked closely together, Gallimore and McGraw would develop a close working relationship and friendship that would last for years.

Over time, Curb and McGraw pulled together the songs they thought were right for the album. Simply titled *Tim McGraw,* the album was released in 1993. Three songs from it were targeted for release as potential single hits. They were "Welcome to the Club," "Memory Lane," and "Two-Steppin' Mind."

But despite high hopes, none of the singles caught on with country-music fans. Although they all made it onto

Tim McGraw (center) stands with record producer Byron Gallimore (left) and musician Darran Smith (right) at the 2004 Country Music Awards. Gallimore not only collaborates professionally with McGraw but is a longtime friend as well.

Billboard's country-music charts, they were too low in the rankings to be considered hits.

Still, McGraw went on a concert tour to promote his work. He was the warm-up act for country-music singer Gene Watson, who was more well known.

Of course, McGraw was disappointed that his first album did not make him a star. But he was not about to give up. Curb, on the other hand, was not so sure. But with the backing of one of Curb's executives, Mike

Billboard Magazine

Billboard is a weekly magazine that tracks single releases and album sales for different kinds of music. It was first published in 1894, with information about such outdoor entertainment events as carnivals, circuses, and fairs. But when the jukebox took off in the 1930s, *Billboard* began to focus on music rankings. By 1961, it only covered the music industry. The magazine ranks singles and albums based on a combination of their sales and the number of times they are played by radio stations.

Borchetta, Curb agreed to give McGraw one more chance.

It prepared to get to work on McGraw's second album. But this time, McGraw wanted to change the process. With his first album, others at Curb Records had taken the lead in choosing the songs. Now, McGraw was determined to take the lead himself. He felt he had good instincts for choosing hit singles. And as things turned out, he was right.

McGraw's second album, *Not a Moment Too Soon,* was released in March 1994. And it surpassed everyone's hopes. Over time, it would sell more than six million copies, and it became *Billboard*'s best-selling country album for 1994. Beyond that, it was the fifth best-selling album that year across all music genres (different kinds of music).

One of the singles on *Not a Moment Too Soon* got McGraw some extra attention. Called "Indian Outlaw," it surprised McGraw by bringing him some negative publicity.

McGraw's band had been performing "Indian Outlaw" for years. He knew it would be a hit because his audiences always responded well to it. But there was a problem with the lyrics. Some American Indians took offense. Wilma Mankiller, chief of the Cherokee Nation, thought the song showed American Indians in a negative way. Some radio stations refused to play the song. Protesters even organized to demonstrate against McGraw and the song at some of his concerts.

McGraw publicly apologized for any unintended offense "Indian Outlaw" may have caused. As he explained, "I wasn't going in to set a political agenda. I wasn't going to try to make a social statement or try to influence anybody. I was just trying to make a good country record."[2]

Chief Wilma Mankiller, pictured here in 2004, objected to the lyrics to Tim McGraw's song "Indian Outlaw" because she felt it stereotyped American Indians. That was not McGraw's intention, and he apologized to the public for any harm the recording may have caused.

Tim McGraw wins "Top New Male Vocalist" at the Academy of Country Music Awards on May 10, 1995.

Still, as they say, all publicity, whether positive or negative, is good publicity. And with "Indian Outlaw," McGraw got the extra publicity boost for his album that it needed. In addition, "Don't Take the Girl," another single from *Not a Moment Too Soon*, became McGraw's first number-one single.

McGraw's mother, Betty, was understandably thrilled with her son's success. "It's just great when your kids succeed in something they really wanted," she would later write.[3] And with the success of *Not a Moment Too Soon*, industry awards quickly followed for McGraw. They highlighted his introduction in Nashville as a rising country-music star. In 1994, McGraw received a Jukebox Award for "Most Played Artist." Betty accepted that one for him. Then he got a lot of national exposure by performing during the Country Music Award (CMA) ceremonies. At the American Music Awards (AMAs) in May, he won the award for "Best New Country Artist." Not surprisingly, he dedicated the award to his mother. And finally, at the Academy of Country Music Awards (ACMs) he won "Top New Male Vocalist" and "Album of the Year."

At last, McGraw's commitment, drive, and hard work had paid off. His career was moving forward in a big way.

 6

Having Faith

The next year, 1995, would be another banner year for Tim McGraw. It included the release of his third album, *All I Want*. Because of the success of his previous album, *Not a Moment Too Soon*, McGraw's ever-increasing fan base was eager for more. More than two million prerelease copies of *All I Want* were sold before the album even hit the stores. Still, not taking anything for granted, McGraw and Curb Records were nervous. Would the new album meet the high expectations everyone had for it?

But they need not have worried. *All I Want* was another home run for McGraw. It quickly sold 2.5

million copies. It also contained two wildly successful single hits. One was "She Never Lets It Go to Her Heart." The other, "I Like It, I Love It," would hit the top of the *Billboard* country chart as a number-one single. And it remained there for five weeks. Later that year, the song would become a part of the sound track for the movie *Something to Talk About,* starring Julia Roberts and Dennis Quaid. Other singles that became big hits from the album were "Can't Really Be Gone," and "All I Want Is a Life." At the 1995 American Music Awards ceremony, McGraw was named "Favorite New Country Artist."

By this time, McGraw had proven his instinct for choosing hit singles. And his band was firmly in place as well. Called the Dancehall Doctors, it was a stable group of talented guys who actually liked one another and got along well. Unlike a lot of bands, where different members come and go from time to time, McGraw's Dancehall Doctors were a strong team. And that was not necessarily easy. As with any band, they spent a lot of time together, not just rehearsing and playing to their fans but also going on their tours. And touring meant living together twenty-four/seven while riding in a cramped bus. They ate together, spent all their tour time together, and missed their families together. It was not an easy life. But the Dancehall Doctors managed to cope and still keep their friendships, despite their continual close contact.[1]

In 1996, McGraw and the Dancehall Doctors began a huge tour to promote his album, *All I Want.* It was called the Spontaneous Combustion tour. This time, McGraw had risen to a level where he was the headlining band, rather than the opening band. He had also worked hard to add drama and excitement to his concert, which now included three huge videos screens and special lighting. McGraw knew his job was to give his audiences all the excitement and energy he could. It was not good enough to just play the songs from his latest album.

The opening act for the tour would be another up-and-coming country-music singer, Faith Hill. For her part, she was promoting her new and very popular album, *It Matters to Me.* As it turned out, the combination of McGraw and Hill would change both of their lives forever.

Faith Hill, or Audrey Faith Perry, was born on September 21, 1967, near Jackson, Mississippi. When she was just one week old, she was adopted by Edna and Ted Perry of Star, Mississippi. When she joined the Perry family, they already had an eight-year-old son, Wesley, and a five-year-old son, Steve. The Perrys adopted Faith because after two boys, Edna wanted to raise a little girl.

Faith Hill's Early Talent

Faith's talent as a singer became obvious very early on. And she loved to sing! When she was just three years old, she belted out hymns with the rest of her church congregation, holding her hymnbook upside down because she could not read yet. When she was seven, she performed at a 4-H mother-daughter luncheon. She also sang at family reunions. But for that, she demanded a price. For smaller events, Edna paid her twenty-five cents. But for bigger family gatherings, Faith upped her price and demanded fifty cents. As she grew older, she was also active in her church choir.

With the Perrys, Faith grew up in a very stable, loving, supportive home. At school, she was active in sports, cheerleading, and, of course, singing. She was heavily influenced by country-music greats, such as Elvis Presley, George Strait, Reba McEntire, and Patsy Cline. Sometimes she would lip-synch to her favorite recordings in the privacy of her bedroom.

She also was very active in her church and came to love gospel music.

When Faith was seventeen, she joined a country-music band. With the band, she was able to get more performing experience by playing for local rodeos, fairs, parties, and church events.

Faith Perry also grew up with a fierce sense of confidence. She would later say, "My mother and father have given me everything. They gave me a backbone, first of all, that has allowed me to be independent and a career woman and a wife and a mother, and I give them full credit for that."[2]

After high school, Faith enrolled briefly at a local community college. But it was not long before she knew that was not her destiny. She needed to follow her dream of becoming a country-music singer. And to do that, she realized she needed to move to Nashville, Tennessee. Just like with Tim McGraw's mother, Betty, Faith's parents were also very supportive of their child's need to follow her dreams, even though they knew her chances of success were not great.

In 1986, when she was just nineteen years old, Faith headed to Nashville. As with McGraw, she knew no one there and had little money. Her main asset, besides her talent, was her high hope for success. She would later reflect on her move by saying, "That is where the wild child in me kicked in. I didn't worry about being safe or where I was going to get money. I just had faith that it was going to work."[3]

Like McGraw, Faith's success in Nashville was not immediate. Her first job there was selling T-shirts at the annual Country Fan Fair. Over time, she found a more permanent job as a secretary/receptionist at Gary Morris Music, a company that published music. In taking that job, Faith was hoping that she would be able to make contacts that could help her get her singing career started.[4]

Faith's job put her in a good position to learn a lot about the music business, which would help her in later years. But much to her frustration, her career hopes did not take off. Still, through her job she met and married Daniel Hill, a music publishing executive, in 1988.

One afternoon, while finishing up her work for the day at Gary Morris Music, thinking that no one else was in the office, Faith Hill began singing. But as luck would have it, songwriter David Chase was still there and heard her. He immediately realized her talent and told her she ought to make a demo tape. Once she did and Gary Morris heard it, he told her to put more effort into getting discovered. With her talent, he thought she was wasting her time working an office job.

Then one night after that, a friend asked Hill to sing backup with her group at the Bluebird Café in Nashville. And as it happened, that night a woman named Martha Sharp was in the audience there. Sharp was a talent scout for Warner Brothers. In fact, she had been responsible for getting Randy Travis signed with Warner Brothers several years earlier.

Sharp was impressed with Hill's performance that night. And when the two met again several days later at a music industry barbeque, she talked to Hill about the possibility of recording for Warner Brothers.

Before long, doors began to open for Hill. With Sharp's recommendation and Hill's extraordinary talent, she signed with Warner Brothers for her first album in 1992. It had taken six years, but Hill was finally pursuing her dream.

Hill's first album, *Take Me As I Am*, was released in the fall of 1993. Pressure on her was huge. It was her one big chance. If the album did not sell well, she might easily have been dropped by Warner Brothers. To help sales,

Hill worked hard to promote her album. Still, although the album was well received by country-music critics, sales fell short of expectations—at least at first. But over time, the album gained momentum.

By the beginning of 1994, one of the singles on the album, "Wild One," skyrocketed to number one on *Billboard*'s country singles chart. And it stayed there for four weeks. That might sound like a pretty short time to most people. But in the music world, with heavy competition from a never-ending onslaught of new singles, it is amazing for a single to hold at number one for that long. After that, another single from the album, "Piece of My Heart," also made it to the top of the country chart.

With two top hit singles from her first album, Hill began getting a lot of attention from the media. She soon made the television circuit, and she was introduced to the general public by appearing on such shows as the *Today* show and *Late Show With David Letterman*. She also began a grueling tour to give *Take Me As I Am* more exposure. As the opening act for more well-known country artists, such as George Strait and Reba McEntire, Hill performed one hundred and fifty times across the United States and Canada. By touring, she got huge exposure for her emerging stardom. And her hard work would pay off. Over time, *Take Me As I Am* sold three million copies.

Faith Hill in 1994.

Despite the hard work and long tours, Hill was ecstatic. "There is nothing like the rush that you feel when you walk out on to that stage," she would later say. "To see all those people cheering for you, to be a part of bringing them so much joy, if for only a couple of hours, is so gratifying."[5]

And not surprisingly, award recognition in the country-music world followed for Faith Hill. In 1994, she was awarded the title of "New Female Vocalist of the Year" by the Academy of Country Music.

Still, her new-found and growing career success was dampened by her marriage, which was falling apart by that time. Hill has always remained private about her reasons for ending her marriage. But she has made it clear it was very difficult for her to admit failure. She had grown up thinking marriage was forever. But looking back, she realized her expectations for marriage had been unrealistic.[6] Once she and Daniel Hill divorced in 1994, she decided to keep her last name of Hill to avoid confusing her fans.

Hill's second album was released in 1995. Called *It Matters to Me*, it became another big success for her. The title single became her fourth number-one hit. And, of course, a new album meant a new tour.

By 1996, Hill had signed on for McGraw's Spontaneous Combustion tour. She would be McGraw's opening act. Hill and McGraw had crossed paths earlier—once in 1994, and later in 1995. "I thought she was gorgeous," McGraw remembered, "but out of my league."[7] For Hill, McGraw also had proven hard to resist. Wearing his signature black cowboy hat and boots, McGraw's appearance could be powerful and intimidating—until he smiled. Then, his tough exterior melted away, replaced by kindness and humor in his eyes.

Working so closely together every day on the tour, sparks began to fly between the two stars. And as they got to know each other better, they also realized they had a lot in common. They had both grown up in the rural South, actually within about twenty miles of each other. They also shared a deep love of family and old-fashioned values.

Still, at the time, Hill was engaged to Scott Hendricks, her song producer. People began to wonder how her budding friendship with McGraw would play out. As her relationship with McGraw became more intense, Hill finally made the tough decision to break her engagement with Hendricks.

As their relationship progressed, McGraw asked Hill to marry him several times. In fact, as Hill remembers, "Tim proposed to me about 50 times in many different ways."[8] But she put him off. After failing at one marriage and another serious relationship, she did not want to make another mistake. But McGraw persisted, refusing to take Hill's "no" for an answer. Finally, she gave him the answer he wanted by scrawling "Yes, I'll be your wife" in marker on his mirror during a concert while he was onstage performing.

By the time the Spontaneous Combustion tour was over, McGraw and Hill had played to audiences in one hundred cities across the nation. The tour had become the highest money-making country-music tour of 1996. The future looked very bright indeed for what was quickly becoming the hottest country-music couple in the country.

> "Tim proposed to me about fifty times in many different ways."

Building on Success

Tim McGraw and Faith Hill were married on October 6, 1996, in Rayville, Louisiana. They kept their plans a big secret. Even the Dancehall Doctors did not know what was going on until the ceremony began. That way, the couple could keep the event solemn and special, without lots of curious and devoted fans causing a distraction. Only a few close friends, family, and the Dancehall Doctors were there. Still, even though the event was quickly planned, there were lots of flowers and a group of musicians to add beauty to the ceremony.

It was held in the back yard of McGraw's Aunt Barbara's home under a big, old oak tree that McGraw had played under as a child. Hill wore a simple white dress and was barefoot. McGraw wore jeans, a long black jacket, and, of course, cowboy boots. His father, Tug, was there, along with McGraw's stepfather, Horace Smith. Faith Hill's adoptive parents, Edna and Ted Perry, and McGraw's mother, Betty, attended as well. During the ceremony, McGraw presented his bride with a huge, five-carat emerald-cut diamond ring. Meanwhile, sheriff's deputies patrolled on the streets outside the house to keep any unexpected onlookers from interfering.

After the ceremony, the newlyweds had work to do. Rather than leaving town for a honeymoon, McGraw and Hill quickly changed into baseball uniforms. Then they headed over to the Tim McGraw Sports Complex there in Rayville. They and the Dancehall Doctors would be playing softball at McGraw's annual Swampstock celebrity softball game. He had started the event two years earlier to give something back to the Rayville community.

Along with the game, there was an auction, followed by a concert. The money they raised would provide scholarships to local youth. It would also help continue to fund a Rayville Little League team. "I began my Swampstock event," McGraw would later explain, "out of a desire to give something back to my hometown community. The kids there needed a place to play ball, a real field. That was never available when I was a child."[1] And since then, Swampstock has continued to raise money for McGraw's projects each year.

For the 1996 Swampstock ball game, McGraw headed up one team. His new wife was captain of the other team. Hill's team won that year, 30–15. During a break in the game, they publicly announced that they had just been married, much to the delight of their fans.

The Spontaneous Combustion tour ended on New Year's Eve 1996 in Nashville, Tennessee. As 1997 dawned, McGraw and Hill faced the new year as the first couple of new country music. There had been other country-music couples throughout the years. They included Conway Twitty and Loretta Lynn, Johnny Cash and June Carter Cash, and George Jones and Tammy Wynette. But except for the Cashes, all the other partnerships were just business. There was no serious romance to provide extra chemistry at their performances. But with the McGraw-Hill union, fans were thrilled with the extra interest and excitement their connection added to the country-music industry.

In addition, McGraw and Hill brought a new country sound to their audiences. Often other influences—sometimes rock, sometimes pop, sometimes gospel—could be heard in their songs. Because of that updated sound, it gave them a broader audience.

Tim McGraw (in the hat) catches a baseball above Chuck Finley, a pitcher for the Anaheim Angels, during the 1999 Swampstock celebrity softball game in Rayville, Louisiana. All proceeds from the game, auction, and concert go to scholarships for local students and funding the town's Little League Baseball team.

Some people who might never have listened to a country-music station could now hear McGraw or Hill on a pop station from time to time. It broadened their appeal and their fan bases, as some of their singles crossed over into other music genres and appeared on more than one *Billboard* chart.

Even so, country-music crossover hits sometimes drew criticism from country-music purists. Some thought that crossover artists were traitors to the heritage and history of true country-music traditions.[2] But McGraw held to his convictions, countering those critics. He said, "I know what I do is country, but I grew up with a lot of influences in music and maybe that shows in my music a little bit. But when it's all said and done, it's definitely country."[3]

"I can't imagine it getting any better. Aside from being able to do something I love for a living, I've got the best wife in the world."

Despite any controversy, McGraw's success was confirmed by the end of 1996. He received nine award nominations from the Academy of Country Music. They included "Entertainer of the Year" and "Album of the Year" for *All I Want*. As McGraw would later reflect, "I can't imagine it getting any better. Aside from being able to do something I love for a living, I've got the best wife in the world."[4]

McGraw's fourth album, *Everywhere*, was released in May 1997. It included a duet with Hill, called "It's Your Love." By September of that year, "It's Your Love" had held *Billboard*'s number-one country slot for six weeks. It was the first country music single in twenty years to hold the number-one place for that long.

McGraw and Hill performed "It's Your Love" at the Academy of Country Music Awards that spring. By September, the song had swept the Country Music Awards by winning "Vocal Event of the Year," "Single of the Year," "Video of the Year," and "Song of the Year." "It's Your Love" also crossed over to the pop charts, winning even more fans and two Grammy nominations. (The Grammy Awards are held each year to recognize outstanding achievements in the recording industry across all music genres.) For his part, McGraw won "Album of the Year" at the Country Music of America Awards for *Everywhere*, which would sell four million copies.

In 1998, McGraw's single, "Just to See You Smile" also hit it big, becoming his second six-week-long number-one single. In fact, five singles from *Everywhere* would make it to the top of *Billboard*'s country-music single chart. And *Everywhere* won "Album of the Year" at the 1998 Academy of Country Music Awards.

Despite his growing celebrity, McGraw still seemed to keep his feet firmly on the ground. He did not let his success go to his head and change his personality. He readily admits that many other country-music singers have better voices than he does.[5] He also thinks the main reason for his popularity is his ability to connect with his fans. He wants them to feel what he feels when he sings. But the main thing he is proud of is his ability to pick songs that become hits. He also likes to test out new singles with his audiences to get their reactions, which he trusts. And his perspective has been confirmed by at least one country-music critic. "When you first hear him, McGraw isn't an obvious candidate for superstardom. Instead of dazzling listeners with roof-shaking [vocal] force, he concentrates on communicating the themes of his songs in a clear, friendly, believable style."[6]

Along with his ability to connect musically with his audiences, McGraw also brings his personal charisma, or charm. With his rugged good looks, one Curb Records executive noted after seeing McGraw perform, "All the girls wanted to date him, the guys wanted to hang out with him, and the women wanted to mother him."[7] It was a powerful combination.

Marriage brought a whole new perspective to McGraw's life, as did fatherhood. His first daughter, Gracie Katherine, was born on May 6, 1997. Hill had known her husband would be good with children. Remembering their premarriage days, she would remark, "I saw this incredible fatherly instinct. . . . He had this real love for children."[8]

McGraw was determined to become the type of father to Gracie that he had not known with his real father, Tug, when he was growing up. And he and Hill set their goals very clearly: Family came first.[9] Still, McGraw's and Hill's careers continued to move forward. Hill's third album, *Faith*, was released in early 1998. To her delight, critics gave the album positive reviews. Among its singles, the album included a duet with McGraw entitled, "Just to Hear You Say That You Love Me."

In March 1998, McGraw and Hill, along with a variety of other country-music singers, joined country-music star George Strait on an eighteen-show tour called the George Strait Country Music Festival. The event combined a variety of carnival rides and games with country-music entertainment. McGraw was Strait's warm-up act. Rather than leaving their daughter behind, McGraw and Hill took Gracie with them. And despite the rigors of a tour, they had a good time. It gave them

Faith Hill sits with two of her daughters during Tim McGraw's induction ceremony into the Hollywood Walk of Fame on October 17, 2006. The oldest daughter, Gracie, is nine and their youngest, Audrey, is four.

time to spend together as a family, as well as the fun of performing for enthusiastic country-music fans.

At the same time, Hill was expecting the couple's second daughter. Maggie Elizabeth would join the McGraw family on August 12, 1998.

That year McGraw also began a tour to promote his latest album, *Everywhere.* This time, Hill stayed home. Yet they were practically newlyweds. They had built a very close relationship, and they had no intention of messing it up. So they made a decision. They would never be apart for more than three nights in a row. They were committed to each other and their family, and they would do whatever it took to keep their strong foundation.

In the spring of 1999, Hill was ready to go on a tour of her own to promote her most recent album, *Faith.* But she was not about to leave her daughters behind. So she baby-proofed her tour bus so it would be ready and safe for them. By the time she was done, it was fitted with bunk beds and a play area for the girls.

Among the singles on *Faith* was a very special one called "This Kiss." It became a huge pop crossover single, and introduced many people who were not familiar with country music to Faith Hill. "This Kiss" became a phenomenal hit for her.

On the downside, the country-music purists were not pleased with "This Kiss." They thought it was too mainstream pop. They actually wanted the song banned from radio playlists. But once fans heard it, they made their wishes clear. Listener requests for the song bombarded radio stations.

"This Kiss" became Hill's most popular song ever—the one that gave her mainstream exposure across America. It became her first single to sell a million copies. And it moved her into a whole new level of recognition. With the success of "This Kiss," Hill became a peer among such music giants as Shania Twain, Mariah Carey, Celine Dion, Whitney Houston, and Alanis Morissette.

Tim McGraw's next album, *A Place in the Sun,* was released in 1999. It sold more than three million copies. It also earned him another "Album of the Year" award at the Country Music Awards. Also in 1999, McGraw began his next tour, called A Place in the Sun. The Dixie Chicks performed as his opening act. Between his own concerts, he also joined George Strait once again for his second Country Music Festival that year.

Faith Hill introduced a new single, "Breathe," at the 1999 Country Music Awards ceremony. Also that year she signed with CoverGirl cosmetics to promote their products on television commercials, and she appeared on the *Divas Live '99* television show with Cher, Tina

Turner, Whitney Houston, and Brandy. The year 1999 was also a winning year for Hill at the Academy of Country Music Awards. She walked away with four major awards, including "Song of the Year" for "This Kiss." McGraw did very well at the same show, winning "Album of the Year" for *A Place in the Sun.* By the end of the year, *Billboard* named McGraw the country's top solo performer for 1999. Its judgment was based on his single and album sales, and the number of times his songs had been played on the radio.

Hill's fourth album, *Breathe,* was released at the end of 1999. It came out just in time for the Christmas shopping season. The album received mixed reviews from critics. Some thought it was not country enough and contained too many crossover songs. Hill admitted the songs on the album had a mix of country, pop, gospel, and rhythm and blues. But the public showed they liked the album a lot. It shot right to the top of *Billboard*'s Top 200 albums.

In the meantime, McGraw and Hill bought 175 acres of land just outside Nashville. With the four-bedroom home they had built on the property, it quickly became their favorite place to be. Along with their home, they added horses and four dogs to keep them company there. McGraw also started a collection of motorcycles.

At home, Hill enjoys her life as queen of the McGraw household. She loves cooking for her family, as well as keeping everyone organized and on schedule. And with her career, her husband's career, and her growing girls, that is a big job.

Despite their talent, Tim McGraw and Faith Hill owe a lot of their success to plain old hard work. Their many tours take an extraordinary amount of time and energy. They have both been eager and willing to increase their exposure with television commercials and small movie parts, along with countless media interviews. They also have popular Web sites for their fans. They both want to reach the largest possible audience and continue to increase their fan bases.

In 2000, McGraw's *Greatest Hits* album was released. It included fifteen of his most popular songs since the start of his career. The album sold close to six million copies, and it was named *Billboard*'s 2001 "Country Album of the Year."

It appeared that life could not be going any better for Tim McGraw. But in June 2000, he had a brief run-in with the law. After a concert in Buffalo, New York, McGraw's friend, country-music singer Kenny Chesney, noticed some of the Buffalo mounted police on their horses. An accomplished rider himself, Chesney asked one of the police officers if he could ride his horse.

Tim McGraw's mother, Betty Trimble, and two of McGraw's daughters watch as McGraw is given a star on the Hollywood Walk of Fame, October 17, 2006. Middle daughter, Maggie (left), is eight. Four-year-old Audrey stands in the center.

The officer agreed, with the condition that Chesney would just sit on the horse and keep it in place. Well, once on the horse, Chesney's instincts took over, and he took off. The police quickly pursued him, at which point McGraw rushed to his friend's defense. He allegedly grabbed one police officer and held him until everything was back under control. For that, he was arrested. McGraw pleaded not guilty, saying, "At no time did I ever throw any punches or put anyone in anything remotely resembling a choke hold."[10] McGraw was released on bail, and the charges were dropped after a trial the following year.

In the last half of 2000, McGraw and Hill embarked on their next tour, called Soul2Soul. Like the Spontaneous Combustion tour, it was extremely successful. They performed in sixty-four cities to sellout crowds. Once again, their tour set records, making the most money of any country-music tour that year.

In 2001, McGraw released his sixth album, *Set This Circus Down*. This was McGraw's favorite album so far. He would later say, "Out of all the records I've made, I feel I'm closest to the mark of the sound and the feel that I had in my head when I wanted to make a record."[11]

Once again, due to prerelease orders, when *Set This Circus Down* hit the stores, it was already at the number-one spot on *Billboard*'s country chart. And in addition to

Faith Hill and Tim McGraw sing a duet during the December 9 concert in Rochester, New York. Their Soul2Soul tour was the most successful country-music tour of 2000.

the release of another award-winning album, 2001 was also special for McGraw and Hill as it marked the arrival of their third daughter, Audrey Caroline, on December 6.

Despite his success, McGraw was not content to sit on his laurels and keep producing the same kinds of songs, just because he knew they would sell well. He was more creative than that and was more interested in pushing the limits by trying new songs, new sounds, and new ideas. And in the next year, he would get that chance.

8

Taking Chances

In 2002, McGraw decided to take on a new and challenging project. He was ready to get to work on his eighth album. But this time, he wanted to try something different. He wanted to record it using the band he had been touring with for years—the Dancehall Doctors.

Now to most people, that might seem to be an odd goal. Had not the Dancehall Doctors recorded all of McGraw's albums with him? The answer is no. Although most albums in other music genres are recorded with the musicians who tour with the band, that was not the case in Nashville. There, when making an album, the singer had to use what they called "session musicians." Those are musicians the recording studio hires to play and to sing backup for their recording artists.

But by 2002, McGraw was ready to stand up against that practice. He thought it was unfair to his band that they were not a part of his albums. He wanted to show his support for them as his longtime and loyal friends. He also wanted their talent to be recognized on an album. "My guys have been with me for a long time and they are an important element of what I do, so it was time to try and capture that on a record," McGraw would later write.[1]

McGraw's keyboardist, Jeff McMahon, would relate, "I think it made some jaws drop when Tim said he was going to use his road band on the record, because that's just not the way things are done in Nashville."[2] Yet, this was not the first time McGraw had bucked Nashville tradition. For years, because of his proven success in picking hit songs, McGraw had insisted on taking the lead in choosing the songs for his albums rather than letting his record company make those decisions. First, he had prevailed against Curb Records by insisting on the inclusion of the single "Indian Outlaw" on his album *Not a Moment Too Soon* in 1994. And that decision had been one of the main reasons for the album's success. Since then, McGraw had developed an excellent reputation in Nashville for being able to hear a demo tape for a single and know if it would be a hit.

In fact, McGraw had also passed over singles that he strongly felt would become hits. Why? Because even though he thought they had a lot of potential, he did not think those songs were right for him and the Dancehall Doctors.[3] As he explained, "[N]o matter how good a song is, if it doesn't feel real to you, it's not going to sound real to other people."[4] That sensitivity and believability had been a big reason for McGraw's connection with his audiences and his resulting success over the years. He was not about to sell out to his audiences by changing that winning formula.

Along those lines, McGraw has also insisted on maintaining his independence and not selling out to the Nashville power brokers in order to promote his career. That is just not the way he works. He has more of a "take-me-or-leave-me" stance, which he has been able to maintain because of his incredible career success. As McGraw has said in that regard, "I've always just tried to be myself and do what feels right for me."[5]

So McGraw proceeded with his idea to record his next album with the Dancehall Doctors. But it would not be as easy as simply having everyone meet at the recording studio and play like they did when they were on tour. As it turns out, playing to an audience at a concert is very different from recording in a studio.

For one thing, when bands perform at concerts, there is a huge and very important interaction that takes place between the musicians and their audience. The two groups play off each other. That dynamic creates an energy that helps the band get into its performance, even though it may have played the same songs countless times at previous concerts. The energy and enthusiasm the band picks up from the audience helps make its performance seem fresh.

But in a recording studio, there are no screaming, adoring fans for the band to see, to hear, and to respond to. Without that, the band members need to get that energy from somewhere else.

To create an album with the Dancehall Doctors would take a lot of determination on McGraw's part. It would also break creative ground for a Nashville album. But McGraw wanted to push the limits and to give it a try. He was not content just to continue on with the same old formula that had brought him so much success already. He wanted to be creative and to try something new. "When we first started this project," McGraw would later write, "I felt like I was doing something good for the band. But actually it turned out that they did something good for me, for themselves and for our

Dancehall Doctors in the Studio

Up until then, it was the recording studio musicians who went through the process of arranging songs. The Dancehall Doctors just heard what McGraw and the studio musicians had recorded. Then they duplicated the arrangements to play for their concerts. Now, McGraw was asking his band to do that up-front work. He wanted them to hear songs and to create arrangements that would appeal to his fans and make the album a hit. It was a tall order.

careers. I feel like this is the greatest music we've ever made together."[6]

If it worked and the album sold well, that would be great. It would prove McGraw's faith in the Dancehall Doctors had been well placed. But if the album fell flat with his fans, it would be a huge failure for McGraw and the Dancehall Doctors. McGraw was taking a big risk. But he intended to use that risk factor as a positive force.

In all, the Dancehall Doctors include eight men. McGraw had found them and pulled them together into a cohesive group that could create the sound he was looking for. And from the first, he did not want to be the big star while his band remained unknown and in the background. He was looking for creative people who could contribute by having good ideas on the direction the band would take. That did not mean they would always agree. But McGraw made it clear from the start that he welcomed new ideas.

Darran Smith is McGraw's lead guitarist, a background singer, and the band leader. Jeff McMahon handles the keyboards, and he is also a background singer. John Marcus plays bass for the band. Bob Minner plays acoustic guitar and banjo. Dean Brown plays fiddle, mandolin, acoustic guitar, cello, and he is yet another background singer. Denny Hemingson also handles

> "When we first started this project, I felt like I was doing something good for the band. But actually it turned out that they did something good for me, for themselves and for our careers. I feel like this is the greatest music we've ever made together."

Tim McGraw (in the cowboy hat) poses with the Dancehall Doctors in front of his star on the Hollywood Walk of Fame. In the front row, left to right: Denny Hemingson, Bob Minner, Tim McGraw, Jeff McMahon. In the back row standing, left to right: Billy Mason, David Dunkley, Darran Smith, John Marcus, Dean Brown.

strings—steel guitar, acoustic guitar, and electric guitar. Billy Mason plays drums for the band, along with David Dunkley, who is also another background singer. The men had all come to Nashville years earlier from across the country. And they all went there with the same hope of making it big in country music.

To begin work on McGraw's eighth album, the first step was to choose the songs. After listening to hundreds of demo tapes of new songs from a variety of song-writers, he and his producers settled on twenty-four semifinalists. At that point, McGraw brought in the Dancehall Doctors to listen, to get their opinions, and to begin experimenting with different arrangements. As a result of that process, the final arrangement of a song might sound completely different than it had on the original demo tape. The band, along with McGraw, spent seven weeks with those songs, evaluating and experimenting before they finally came up with the ones they thought would work for the album.

The next big move for McGraw was to take the Dancehall Doctors somewhere besides a standard Nashville recording studio to get the songs recorded. He not only wanted his band in a different environment, he wanted to take them out of Nashville. That way, they would be away from all the pressures of their lives at home, and they would be more able to put all their attention and creativity into making the best possible album. "Working in the studio can get a little stale, and for this project we wanted to create a comfortable atmosphere that would encourage creativity and inspiration," he later explained.[7]

After searching the country for the kind of fresh environment he was looking for, McGraw chose Allaire Studio in upstate New York. It was a recording studio in the Catskill Mountains that had been converted from an old farmhouse. Away from civilization, the only way to get to it was on a ten-mile-long, narrow, winding road.

Besides themselves, the Dancehall Doctors had a lot of equipment to transport to the studio. It completely filled a fifty-three-foot-long truck. As part of its cargo, the truck included a dozen amplifiers, several drum sets, and as many as seventy guitars.

Before they got there, McGraw had hired a person to turn the studio into the most relaxing and comfortable environment possible. He covered the floors with oriental rugs and placed candles everywhere. Each of the band members was given pens and pads of paper so they could write about their experiences, along with any spur-of-the-moment ideas they might have. He also had video games installed to give them added relaxation and a way to blow off steam and to have fun. McGraw related, "I wanted our comfort level to be so high that everybody would feel comfortable voicing their opinion and trying things and not being afraid of messing up."[8]

McGraw and the Dancehall Doctors worked and recorded at the Allaire studio for eleven days. When they started out, their goal had been to record six songs. Instead, they came away with seventeen. It had been a very successful trip.

After finishing their recording experiment, the Dancehall Doctors headed out on the road again for a summer 2002 tour. While on tour, they tried out some of the songs that would be on the new album. McGraw was pleased with the results. He would later write: "The guys in my band have always played their hearts out on stage. . . . But when we play the new songs live now, the vibe is different, because the guys are playing parts they created, rather than other people's parts that they learned off a record."[9]

So, how did the album do? Did McGraw's big risk pay off? It did. Upon its release, *Tim McGraw and the Dancehall Doctors* jumped to the number-two slot on *Billboard*'s country album chart. It also spun off several singles that became solid hits, including "Real Good Man," "She's My Kind of Rain," and "Red Rag Top."

Along with the album's release, a book called *Tim McGraw and the Dancehall Doctors: This Is Ours* hit bookstores. The book describes the process the band went through to create the album and includes lots of pictures of McGraw and his band.

Success seemed to follow everything McGraw did. In addition, he and his wife had built a very strong marriage that could withstand the special challenges of celebrity. Yet McGraw had never taken his success for granted. Since the beginning of Swampstock, he had always been interested in giving something of his growing success back to his fans. As time would reveal, that opportunity would soon present itself, and McGraw would rise to the challenge.

Celebrity With a Heart

In the spring of 2003, McGraw's father, Tug, was working with the pitching staff for the Philadelphia Phillies in Coldwater, Florida. He had retired from his baseball career, but he still had a lot to offer as a consultant to the team, based on his many years of experience as a player. Always known as a fun-loving guy, Tug enjoyed kidding around and making people laugh. But his life was soon to turn very serious.

As the spring progressed, Tug became alarmed. All of a sudden, his behavior was changing in ways he could not control. For one thing, he had less energy than usual. And then his speech was odd. Without warning he found himself stuttering or forgetting his thoughts in mid-sentence. Sometimes he would make off-the-wall comments and not know why. He was confused and had no idea what was going on. It was very unsettling. He thought perhaps he had had a stroke, a medical condition in which a blood vessel in the brain gets blocked or bursts. Without oxygen from the blood, parts of the brain can quickly become damaged, leading to physical and/or mental disability.

Tug's symptoms were alarming and took him by surprise. He finally decided to get to a hospital to find out what was going on. As it turned out, Tug's problems were worse than he had imagined. After being admitted to a hospital in Coldwater for tests, Tug was stunned with his diagnosis. He had two fast-growing cancerous tumors in his brain. And the news got worse from there. His condition was not treatable. He only had weeks to live. He was just fifty-nine years old.

Stunned, Tug contacted his family immediately, including his son, Tim. At the time, Tim McGraw was at home in Nashville. He would soon be starting a concert tour in Florida. But with Tug's call, his son immediately rushed to Coldwater to see how he could help his father.

Even though Tug and Tim McGraw had never had a very close relationship, his father's death in early 2004 hit McGraw hard. He would write: "I never called him

Dad, but I think I will miss him as though I had him all along. Strange how that works." He would also write to his father, "Go rest. Me and you—we're OK."[1] And as McGraw's longtime friend and record producer Byron Gallimore observed, "Tim keeps a lot of things to himself. But seeing his father die at a relatively young age shook him badly."[2]

Shortly after Tug died, McGraw recorded his ninth album. It was called *Live Like You Were Dying*. He dedicated the title song to his father. In reflecting on the recording experience at such a difficult time in his life, McGraw said, "It was probably therapeutic. Dad died the first week in January, and at the end of that month I was in the studio recording with all my best friends. It was a good chance to get up there and blow all that stuff off, blow it into the music."[3]

As with his previous album, *Tim McGraw and the Dancehall Doctors*, McGraw recorded *Live Like You Were Dying* with his touring band, the Dancehall Doctors. First, they spent eight weeks working on the album in a Nashville warehouse. Then they returned to their retreat in the Catskill Mountains in upstate New York to get the songs recorded.

The title single from the album, "Live Like You Were Dying," became a huge hit; the biggest of McGraw's career.[4] As a tribute to his father and to anyone who faces

Tug McGraw appears optimistic during a news conference on May 29, 2003, despite having just had surgery to remove a brain tumor. Sadly, he lost his battle with brain cancer on January 5, 2004, at the age of fifty-nine.

an untimely death, the song encourages its listeners to live each day to the fullest, to take risks, and to make the most of each day. The song's message is that life is fragile and should not be taken for granted. Because no one knows when his or her life will come to an end.

The song had been written by Tim Nichols and Craig Wiseman. Along with the release of the album, an inspirational book by the same title hit bookstores. It included a compact disc with McGraw's single. It also contained a forward by McGraw. He wrote: "I hope this song can provide inspiration for all of us to stop and take time to appreciate all the blessings in our lives—from the smallest things to the biggest dreams."[5]

With this album, McGraw got huge media exposure. He also went on the interview circuit to promote it, including appearances on such television shows as *Good Morning America, The Tonight Show With Jay Leno,* and *The View.*

Later in 2004, McGraw branched out creatively once again. This time, he teamed up with rap artist Nelly (Cornell Haynes, Jr.). Nelly was a superstar in the world of rap music—quite a different genre from country music. Still, the two men created a hit called "Over and Over." Nelly included it on his rhythm and blues album, *Suit.* The single became a crossover hit, straddling *Billboard*'s country and hip-hop charts.

Then McGraw surfaced again in an entirely new artistic area—acting. His first venture was a movie called *Friday Night Lights,* released in August 2004. The movie was about a high school football team, the Permian Panthers of Odessa, Texas. Odessa had hit hard times, with a declining population and a tough economy. The one positive focus that rallied the town was its

McGraw performs with Nelly on the 2004 television special *Tim McGraw: Here and Now.*

football team. Academy Award–winning actor Billy Bob Thornton played the Panthers' coach, Gary Gaines. McGraw played a supporting part very different from his real life—as an abusive father with an addiction to alcohol.

The next year brought McGraw to the big screen once again. Released to theaters in March 2005, the movie was called *Black Cloud*. Set in the American southwest, it was a story about a young American Indian named Black Cloud. He was struggling to come to grips with his heritage. The film was written and directed by Rick Schroeder, and McGraw played the role of the town sheriff who became involved when Black Cloud got into trouble with the law.

It looked like 2005 would be yet another great year for Tim McGraw. But the month of August would rock him, his wife, and all Americans to their cores. Because that was the month Hurricane Katrina struck New Orleans, Louisiana—the largest city in the state and where McGraw had grown up.

New Orleans is located at the mouth of the Mississippi River, where it empties into the Gulf of Mexico. Founded in 1718, it is one of the oldest cities in the United States. The city is beloved by many Americans. It is famous for its French culture, heritage, architecture, and cuisine (cooking). The city is also

Tim McGraw makes his acting debut in the 2004 film *Friday Night Lights*, playing the role of Charles Billingsley, an abusive alcoholic who does not believe his son, Don (Garrett Hedlund), is as dedicated to football as Charles was in high school.

generally recognized as the birthplace of jazz music. In addition, New Orleans is famous for its annual pre-Easter Mardi Gras festivities, which attract visitors from across the country. During the years, New Orleans has become popular with tourists and as a favorite site for business conventions.

Still, there was a problem. The city of New Orleans was built on lowlands. In fact, over time many parts of the city had actually sunk so that they were below sea level. So how did New Orleans keep the nearby ocean from overrunning the city? It faced the challenge by building a system of levees, or walls. They were either earthen or concrete, and they were critical in keeping the ocean waters at bay and the city dry.

Over the years, the New Orleans levee system had worked pretty well. In 1965, a fierce storm, Hurricane Betsy, hit the city hard. Even so, only 20 percent of the city flooded; 80 percent remained dry.

But 2005 would be a very different story. Everyone knew that Hurricane Katrina was coming, with New Orleans in her sights. In response, most of the city's population of almost 375,000 people evacuated to other places and higher ground. But many of the citizens of New Orleans did not have a way to escape. Their best choice was to head downtown to New Orleans's Superdome athletic complex. With the hurricane rapidly approaching, as many as twenty-six thousand New Orleans citizens went to the Superdome seeking shelter. It was considered a refuge of last resort. People heading there were told to bring their own food, water, and supplies. Some did; many did not.

Still, that haven of safety turned out to be a living nightmare. Unable to handle so many people, the facility became dreadfully overcrowded. Then, once Katrina hit, electricity and water service failed. There was not enough food, water, or bathrooms to handle the huge crowd. Even crime became a problem, with some people terrorizing helpless victims. And before the hurricane was over, the Superdome itself was damaged, with big pieces of the building's roof torn off.

By the time Katrina blew herself out and the damage could be assessed, more than fifteen hundred people had died in Louisiana. Most of them were in New Orleans.

Hurricane Katrina

As a Category Three hurricane, Hurricane Katrina hit New Orleans hard. And with the fury of the storm, the city's levee system was no match. The levees were either breached, meaning the water got so high it went over the levees, or they broke entirely from the tremendous force and power of the water. With that, 80 percent of the city of New Orleans was flooded.

On top of that, hundreds of thousands of New Orleans citizens were now displaced. With their homes and businesses flooded, they had no place to return to. Many were put in temporary housing in the cities that had welcomed people fleeing from the storm. But even after two years had passed, estimates showed that at least one-third of the city's original population still had not moved back to the city.

Tim McGraw had grown up in Louisiana. Even though he now lived in Tennessee, Louisiana still remained close to his heart. He and Hill, along with many Americans, were particularly touched and grieved by the devastation the state had endured. So McGraw and Hill decided to do what they could to help. First, they participated in an effort to get food and other supplies to the area. Then they established an organization called the Neighbor's Keeper Foundation. Its purpose is to raise money to assist victims of natural disasters.

And that was not all. McGraw headlined a concert shortly after the hurricane. It was called *A Concert for Hurricane Relief*. It aired on NBC, MSNBC, and CNBC to raise money for the American Red Cross Disaster Relief Fund. Celebrity musicians Harry Connick, Jr., and Wynton Marsalis also participated in the benefit concert. Regarding the event, McGraw said, "I am

Tim McGraw speaks at a news conference near New Orleans, Louisiana, on November 29, 2005, exactly three months after Hurricane Katrina devastated the Gulf Coast. He informed the media that he was teaming up with other celebrities and Amazon.com to raise money for the disaster victims.

heartbroken by the devastation caused by Hurricane Katrina in my home state. Like so many Americans I am watching the news reports with great sadness. But it's at times like these that each of us must work together to provide lifesaving aid to those in terrible need."[6]

Meanwhile, Tim McGraw's career had been on a steady rise since he first got major attention in 1993. But he was not about to rest on that success. He had many new ventures ahead. And he was up for the challenge.

> "I am heartbroken by the devastation caused by Hurricane Katrina in my home state. Like so many Americans I am watching the news reports with great sadness. But it's at times like these that each of us must work together to provide lifesaving aid to those in terrible need."

Looking to the Future

In 2006, Tim McGraw and Faith Hill headed back out on tour again. Building on the success of their earlier Soul2Soul tour in 2000, this one was called Soul2Soul II.

Lots of people attend music concerts, but few have any idea what goes into creating one. The planning for a tour can take a year—or more. Experts are hired to create the stage design, or a series of designs that will become backdrops throughout the concert. Then there is choreography—either actual dance routines or, at a minimum, the decisions on where all the performers will stand on the stage and where they will move as the concert progresses. Ticket sales and concert dates have to be organized and coordinated, along with transportation logistics for the many people who will make the concert happen.

Attention must also be paid to any competitive bands that may be touring at the same time. That way, each artist has the greatest chance of drawing the biggest possible audience. Special lighting has become a huge issue at concerts. It adds to the show's drama and helps energize the fans. On top of that, gigantic video screens are almost always a part of a concert, so that everyone in the audience feels close to the band no matter where they may be sitting. And the whole complex operation has to be set up quickly night after night, in ever-different arenas.

To make the Soul2Soul II tour work, McGraw and Hill also had to bring their separate management teams together. McGraw was managed by Scott Siman out of Nashville. Hill was managed by a firm from Los Angeles, California. And both management teams had their own ideas about how to put together the most effective tour for their clients. All together, the Soul2Soul II tour required at least a year and a half to plan.

In addition to all the pre-tour planning, it is critical that the whole production comes off flawlessly to the audience. After all, everyone there has probably paid

Family First

The Soul2Soul II tour had yet another complication. All the tour dates had to be scheduled on weekends, because McGraw and Hill insisted on planning their tour around their three children's school schedules.

quite a bit of money for their tickets. They expect a great performance, and they expect everything to run smoothly. It takes a lot of skilled technicians to pull that off night after night during a tour. In fact, the Soul2Soul II tour needed sixteen trucks to haul all the tour equipment from city to city. And as for the number of people needed to make Soul2Soul II happen each night? A whopping one hundred and forty-four![1]

The Soul2Soul II tour also had a fresh, new look. "We never do anything unless we want it to be the biggest and the best thing out there," McGraw said in terms of the plans for the tour.[2] So this time, the show was performed in the round. That way, the only stage background is the audience on the other side of the arena. "We wanted to

On July 5, 2006, McGraw performs in New Orleans during the Soul2Soul II tour. The money from the concert went to McGraw and Hill's Neighbor's Keepers Foundation to help Hurricane Katrina victims.

do it in the round because we felt like it was a different experience," McGraw would comment. "It brings us closer to the audience."[3]

The Soul2Soul II tour began in spring 2006 in Columbus, Ohio. This would be McGraw and Hill's third time to tour together. And their fans were more than ready to see them together again. Playing seventy-four shows in fifty-six cities, the tour would not end until September.

And as it turned out, all the planning and preparation for the tour paid off. It brought in more money than any tour in the history of country music, and it was one of the top five tours that year for any music genre.[4]

In October 2006, McGraw's third movie was released to theaters across the country. Called *Flicka*, it was based on the 1941 children's book *My Friend Flicka*, by Mary O'Hara. The movie is about a sixteen-year-old girl, Katy, who has dreams of managing her father's horse ranch. Tim McGraw plays Katy's father. The film also included a McGraw song, "My Little Girl," as part of its sound track.

The family-friendly movie did respectably at the box office. But it did even better in the DVD market, making $67 million between DVD sales and rentals—another success for McGraw to add to his long, long list of profitable projects.

Tim McGraw plays a horse rancher in the 2006 children's movie *Flicka*.

After that, the Soul2Soul II tour of 2006 was extended into 2007. But McGraw and Hill both realized it might be their final joint tour. As McGraw looked to the future, he said, "[T]his will probably be the last year we can both go out. Our [children are] starting to get their friends—they're starting to get their own lives. So that's why we decided, 'Let's go out one more year together, because we might never be able to do it again.'"[5]

McGraw's eleventh album, *Let It Go*, was released in March 2007. It immediately shot to number one on

Billboard's country-music album chart. The album also contained five singles that would make it onto *Billboard*'s "Top 20 Hot Country Songs" chart. Hill joined McGraw on two songs on the album, with "I Need You" and "Shotgun Rider." In addition, McGraw branched out by joining two other songwriters, Brad and Brent Warren, to create two of the album's singles, "Train #10" and "If You're Reading This." ("If You're Reading This" was added to a second release of the album.) "If You're Reading This" made it to number three on the country charts, and McGraw performed the song at the 2007 Academy of Country Music Awards ceremony.

In September 2007, McGraw's fourth movie was released. This one, called *The Kingdom,* was a big change from McGraw's earlier feel-good, family movies. An action drama, the movie was about a terrorist attack on an American facility in the kingdom of Saudi Arabia and the resulting effort to bring the attackers to justice. Along with McGraw, the movie starred Jamie Foxx, Jennifer Garner, and Jason Bateman.

McGraw's next tour, Live Your Voice, began in May 2008 in Tampa, Florida. This time Hill stayed at home with the girls. The tour ended on July 6 in Pittsburgh, Pennsylvania, having played to almost 500,000 fans.

Also in 2008, McGraw added to his accomplishments with the release of his first book in October. Titled *My*

Little Girl, the book is for children and is about the close bond between a father and his daughter. The book also includes a foreword by Faith Hill. It was written by McGraw, with the help of songwriter Tom Douglas, after Douglas wrote the song for McGraw by the same title. The book shows McGraw's love for his children and his longtime commitment to keeping his family as the first priority in his life.

McGraw and Tom Douglas hold copies of *My Little Girl* at a book signing in New York on October 23, 2008.

McGraw's exposure has also broadened with a number of Tim McGraw products that have become available to buy. Besides his children's book, he has released Tim McGraw calendars for a number of years. And along with the usual array of T-shirts, mugs, posters, baseball caps, baby clothes, and mouse pads sold at his concerts and on his Web site, he also launched a new men's cologne called "McGraw by Tim McGraw" in August 2008.

In late 2008, McGraw's fifth movie was released. Called *Four Christmases*, the comedy/drama revolves around the hoops one couple goes through as they visit their family's four separate households on Christmas Day. Along with McGraw in a supporting role, the movie has an award-winning cast, including Vince Vaughn, Reese Witherspoon, and Robert Duvall. The end of 2008 also saw the release of McGraw's next album, *Greatest Hits 3*.

The following year, McGraw acted with Sandra Bullock in *The Blind Side*. The film, based on a 2006 book by Michael Lewis, is about the early life of professional football player Michael Oher, offensive tackle for the Baltimore Ravens. Oher overcame poverty and gained a successful career playing football with the help of his adoptive parents, played by McGraw and Bullock.

Tim McGraw poses with his cologne, named "McGraw," in New York on April 29, 2008.

So what has catapulted McGraw to superstardom over such a long period of time? Probably not his singing talent. At least not that alone. As he himself has admitted, he is a good singer, but not spectacular. His rugged look is appealing and probably accounts for some of his fans. And his hard work and devotion to his art have definitely moved his career forward. But overall, it seems that his phenomenal success is the result of his authenticity and sincerity that help him reach his fans on a deep level. They believe in him, they believe they understand him, they respect him, and they always support him.

In addition, McGraw has a strong family to cheer him on. In a world where long-lasting celebrity marriages are rare, McGraw and Hill seem to have beaten the odds. Celebrity marriages can flounder because of differing goals, hectic travel schedules, and even career competition. But McGraw and Hill appear to have successfully overcome those obstacles.

McGraw continues supporting charitable causes as well. Swampstock remains an annual event in Rayville, Louisiana. The Neighbor's Keeper Foundation continues to raise money for those in need. McGraw still holds his position on the American Red Cross National Celebrity Cabinet. And he has also helped Brett Favre—famous quarterback for the National Football League—with his Favre Forward Foundation, which benefits disabled children in Wisconsin and Mississippi.

So, what lies ahead for Tim McGraw? After all he has accomplished, has he reached the top of his career? Well, as it turns out, he believes he is just hitting his stride and still has a lot of work to do. "I feel that I'm learning all the time. And I think that I'm just now starting to get a hold on what I do."[6]

Besides his incredible success as a country-music superstar, McGraw has also shown some interest in jumping from the concert stage into the political arena. "Public service is a pretty high calling. If I felt like I could do some good, if I felt I had the brains and maturity someday, then it's something I would consider—after my kids were grown," McGraw has said.[7]

> **"I feel that I'm learning all the time. And I think that I'm just now starting to get a hold on what I do."**

Still, looking to the future, McGraw is a realist. He realizes his career cannot go on forever. But as he puts it, "[A]s long as I can fit in these jeans, and as long as people come to me, come to see us, we'll be doing it."[8] And there are a lot of McGraw fans who are counting on that.

Chronology

1967—Samuel Timothy McGraw is born on May 1 in Delhi, Louisiana; Tim's mother, Betty D'Agostino, marries Horace Smith.

1977—Betty and Horace Smith divorce.

1978—McGraw discovers that his real father is Frank Edwin "Tug" McGraw, Jr., famous baseball pitcher.

1985—McGraw enrolls at Northeast Louisiana University with a music scholarship.

1989—McGraw leaves college to pursue music career in Nashville, Tennessee.

1992—McGraw signs with Curb Records; releases his first single, "Welcome to the Club."

1993—McGraw's first album, *Tim McGraw* is released in April.

1994—McGraw's second album, *Not a Moment Too Soon*, is released; McGraw begins his annual Swampstock celebrity softball game and concert in Rayville, Louisiana, to raise money for Rayville's Little League team.

1995—McGraw's third album, *All I Want*, is released.

1996—McGraw launches his Spontaneous Combustion tour with Faith Hill as his opening act; McGraw and Hill are married on October 6.

1997—McGraw's first child, Gracie Katherine, is born; McGraw's fourth album, *Everywhere*, is released.

1998—McGraw's second child, Maggie Elizabeth, is born.

1999—McGraw's fifth album, *A Place in the Sun*, is released.

2000—McGraw's sixth album, *Greatest Hits*, is released; McGraw and Hill launch their Soul2Soul tour.

2001—McGraw's third child, Audrey Caroline, is born; McGraw's seventh album, *Set This Circus Down*, is released.

2002—McGraw defies Nashville tradition by recording his eighth album, *Tim McGraw and the Dancehall Doctors*, using his touring band rather than recording studio musicians.

2004—McGraw's father, Tug McGraw, dies of cancer in January; McGraw's ninth album, *Live Like You Were Dying*, is released; McGraw has a supporting role in the movie *Friday Night Lights*.

2005—Hurricane Katrina strikes the southern United States; McGraw joins other musicians in a benefit concert to raise money for Katrina victims; McGraw appears in his second movie, *Black Cloud*.

2006—McGraw releases his tenth album, *Greatest Hits, Vol. 2*; McGraw and Hill conduct Soul2Soul II tour; McGraw appears in his third movie, *My Friend Flicka.*

2007—The Soul2Soul II tour continues; McGraw's eleventh album, *Let It Go*, is released; McGraw appears in his fourth movie, *The Kingdom.*

2008—McGraw launches his Live Your Voice tour; first book, *My Little Girl*, is published; McGraw's fifth movie, *Four Christmases*, is released.

2009—McGraw's sixth movie, *The Blind Side*, is released.

Discography

Albums

1993 *Tim McGraw*

1994 *Not a Moment Too Soon*

1995 *All I Want*

1997 *Everywhere*

1999 *A Place in the Sun*

2000 *Greatest Hits*

2001 *Set This Circus Down*

2002 *Tim McGraw and the Dancehall Doctors*

2004 *Live Like You Were Dying*

2006 *Tim McGraw Reflected: Greatest Hits, Volume 2*

2007 *Let It Go*

2008 *Greatest Hits: Limited Edition*

Collector's Edition

Greatest Hits 3

Limited Edition: Greatest Hits, Volumes 1, 2, & 3

2009 *Southern Voice*

Collaborative Singles

1998 *"Just to Hear You Say That You Love Me"* [with Faith Hill]

2000 *"Let's Make Love"* [with Faith Hill]

2001 *"Bring on the Rain"* [with Joe Dee Messina]

2004 *"Over and Over"* [with Nelly]

2008 *"Nine Lives"* [with Def Leppard]

Filmography

2004	*Black Cloud*
2004	*Friday Night Lights*
2006	*Flicka*
2007	*The Kingdom*
2008	*Four Christmases*
2009	*The Blind Side*

Chapter Notes

Chapter 1
A Chance Encounter

1. Tug McGraw, with Don Yaeger, *Ya Gotta Believe: My Roller-Coaster Life as a Screwball Pitcher and Part-Time Father, and My Hope-Filled Fight Against Brain Cancer* (New York: New American Library, 2004), p. 1.
2. Scott Gray, *Perfect Harmony* (New York: Ballantine Books, 1999), p. 2.

Chapter 2
Growing Up Timmy

1. Tug McGraw, with Don Yaeger, *Ya Gotta Believe: My Roller-Coaster Life as a Screwball Pitcher and Part-Time Father, and My Hope-Filled Fight Against Brain Cancer* (New York: New American Library, 2004), p. 125.
2. Betty Trimble, "McMom," *Tim McGraw: A Mother's Story* (Nashville, Tenn.: D'Agostino/Dahlhauser/Ditmore Publishing, 1996), p. 37.
3. Ibid., p. 50.
4. Ibid., p. 48.
5. Ibid., pp. 46–48.
6. Ibid., pp. 53–54.
7. Ibid.
8. Jeremy K. Brown, "Tim McGraw," *Current Biography*, September 2002, pp. 1–2.
9. Trimble, p. 61.
10. Ibid., pp. 57–58, 61–62, 67–68.
11. Ibid., p. 81.
12. Jim Brown, *Faith Hill and Tim McGraw: Soul 2 Soul* (Kingston, Ontario: Quarry Music Books, 2002), p. 19.
13. Trimble, pp. 94–96

14. Christopher John Farley, "Tennessee Two-Step," *Time*, June 28, 1999, p. 69.
15. Trimble, p. 91.
16. Ibid., p. 96.

Chapter 3
A Secret Revealed

1. Betty Trimble, "McMom," *Tim McGraw: A Mother's Story* (Nashville, Tenn.: D'Agostino/Dahlhauser/Ditmore Publishing, 1996), p. 107.
2. Tug McGraw, with Don Yaeger, *Ya Gotta Believe: My Roller-Coaster Life as a Screwball Pitcher and Part-Time Father, and My Hope-Filled Fight Against Brain Cancer* (New York: New American Library, 2004), pp. 129–130.
3. Ibid., p. 132.
4. Ibid., p. 133.
5. Trimble, p. 126.
6. McGraw, p. 157.
7. Ibid., p. 158.
8. Ibid.

Chapter 4
A Change of Plans

1. Jim Brown, *Faith Hill and Tim McGraw: Soul 2 Soul* (Kingston, Ontario: Quarry Music Books, 2002), p. 26.
2. Ibid.
3. Ibid.
4. Tug McGraw, with Don Yaeger, *Ya Gotta Believe: My Roller-Coaster Life as a Screwball Pitcher and Part-Time Father, and My Hope-Filled Fight Against Brain Cancer* (New York: New American Library, 2004), p. 162.
5. Betty Trimble, "McMom," *Tim McGraw: A Mother's Story* (Nashville, Tenn.: D'Agostino/Dahlhauser/Ditmore Publishing, 1996), pp. 159–161.
6. Brown, p. 27.
7. Trimble, p. 171.
8. Brown, p. 27.

Chapter Notes

....

Chapter 5
Building a Career

1. Tug McGraw, with Don Yaeger, *Ya Gotta Believe: My Roller-Coaster Life as a Screwball Pitcher and Part-Time Father, and My Hope-Filled Fight Against Brain Cancer* (New York: New American Library, 2004), p. 168.
2. Mike Joyce, "McGraw Makes Right Plays," *Washington Post*, November 25, 1994, cited in Jeremy K. Brown, "Tim McGraw," *Current Biography*, September 2002, p. 3.
3. Betty Trimble, "McMom," *Tim McGraw: A Mother's Story* (Nashville, Tenn.: D'Agostino/Dahlhauser/Ditmore Publishing, 1996), p. 184.

Chapter 6
Having Faith

1. Jim Brown, *Faith Hill and Tim McGraw: Soul 2 Soul* (Kingston, Ontario: Quarry Music Books, 2002), p. 122.
2. Ibid., p. 31
3. Ibid., p. 41.
4. Scott Gray, *Perfect Harmony* (New York: Ballantine Books, 1999), p. 128.
5. "Bio," *Faith Hill*, 2009, <http://www.faithhill.com/site.php?content=bio> (June 1, 2009).
6. Brown, pp. 66–67.
7. Jeremy Helligar and Lorna Grisby, "Song: Hunky Tonk Singer Tim McGraw Conquers Fatherhood and Nashville," *People*, April 27, 1998, p. 1.
8. "Love at First Sight," *Country Weekly*, February 25, 2008, p. 36.

Chapter 7
Building on Success

1. Beth Johnson, "10 Famous Fathers Put Children First: Tim McGraw," *Parents.com*, n.d., <http://www.parents.com/family-life/celebrity-parents/moms-dads/10-famous-fathers-put-children-first/?page=7> (July 1, 2009).
2. Jim Brown, *Faith Hill and Tim McGraw: Soul 2 Soul* (Kingston, Ontario: Quarry Music Books, 2002), p. 121.
3. Ibid., p. 122.

4. Jeremy Helligar and Lorna Grisby, "Song: Hunky Tonk Singer Tim McGraw Conquers Fatherhood and Nashville," *People*, April 27, 1998, p. 1.

5. Jim Brown, p. 120.

6. Jeremy K. Brown, "Tim McGraw," *Current Biography*, September 2002, p. 1.

7. Tug McGraw, with Don Yaeger, *Ya Gotta Believe: My Roller-Coaster Life as a Screwball Pitcher and Part-Time Father, and My Hope-Filled Fight Against Brain Cancer* (New York: New American Library, 2004), p. 168.

8. Helligar and Grisby, p. 1.

9. Scott Gray, *Perfect Harmony* (New York: Ballantine Books, 1999), p. 195.

10. Jeremy Brown, p. 4.

11. Ibid.

Chapter 8

Taking Chances

1. Tim McGraw, with Martin Huxley, *This Is Ours: Tim McGraw and the Dancehall Doctors* (New York: Atria Books, 2002), p. 4.

2. Ibid., p. 9.

3. Ibid., p. 67.

4. Ibid.

5. Ibid., p. 44.

6. Ibid., frontmatter.

7. Ibid., p. 97.

8. Ibid., pp. 117–118.

9. Ibid., p. 153.

Chapter 9

Celebrity With a Heart

1. Tug McGraw, with Don Yaeger, *Ya Gotta Believe: My Roller-Coaster Life as a Screwball Pitcher and Part-Time Father, and My Hope-Filled Fight Against Brain Cancer* (New York: New American Library, 2004), p. ix.

2. Mike Lipton, "Playing Through the Pain," *People*, August 30, 2004, p. 83.

3. Deborah Evans Price, "McGraw Tugs Heart Strings," *Billboard*, August 28, 2004, p. 5.

4. Ibid.
5. Tim Nichols and Craig Wiseman, *Live Like You Were Dying* (Nashville, Tenn.: Rutledge Hill Press, 2004), Foreward.
6. "Tim McGraw to Headline NBC Concert in Support of Hurricane Katrina Victims," PR *Newswire*, August 31, 2005, <http://www.prnewswire.com/cgi-bin/stories.pl?ACCT=104& STORY=/www/story/08-31-2005/0004097773&EDATE=#> (July 1, 2009).

Chapter 10

Looking to the Future

1. Ray Waddell and Tamara Conniff, "Tim and Faith: On the Road," *Billboard*, July 8, 2006, p. 4.
2. Ibid., p. 2.
3. Ibid.
4. "Tim McGraw Biography," *Curb.com*, n.d., <http://www.curb.com/artists/artistbio_T1.cfm?ID=33> (June 1, 2009).
5. Lori Berger, "Love and Faith . . .That's the Secret to the Life They Love (American Country Singers Faith Hill and Tim McGraw)," *Redbook*, July 1, 2007, p. 128.
6. Dave DiMartino, "A Lot to Live For," *Yahoo! Music*, March 10, 2008, <http://ca.music.yahoo.com/read/interview/14129756> (June 1, 2009).
7. Karen S. Schneider and Natasha Stoynoff, "Tim and Faith: Heart to Heart," *People*, July 17, 2006, p. 95.
8. DiMartino, p. 3.

Further Reading

Brown, Jim. *Faith Hill and Tim McGraw: Soul 2 Soul.* Kingston, Ontario, Canada: Quarry Music Books, 2002.

McGraw, Tim, with Martin Huxley. *Tim McGraw and the Dancehall Doctors: This Is Ours.* New York: Atria Books, 2006.

McGraw, Tug, with Don Yaeger. *Ya Gotta Believe! My Roller-Coaster Life as a Screwball Pitcher and Part-Time Father, and My Hope-Filled Fight Against Brain Cancer.* New York: Penguin Group, Inc., 2004.

Medlock Adams, Michelle. *Tim McGraw.* Hockessin, Del.: Mitchell Lane, 2007.

Internet Addresses

Tim McGraw Official Web Site
http://www.timmcgraw.com

Faith Hill Official Web Site
http://www.faithhill.com

Neighbor's Keeper Foundation
http://www.neighborskeeper.org/

Index

Index